HATFIELD
AND ITS PEOPLE

THE STORY OF A NEW TOWN, A GARDEN CITY,
AN OLD VILLAGE, A HISTORIC HOUSE, THE
FARMS AND THE COUNTRYSIDE
IN A HERTFORDSHIRE PARISH

discovered and related by
the
HATFIELD W.E.A.

(Members of the Hatfield Local History Tutorial Class of
Cambridge University Extra-Mural Board, organized by the
Hatfield Branch of the Workers' Educational Association, under
the tutorship of
Lionel M. Munby, M.A.)

PART 5

ROADS AND RAILWAYS
and Population Changes

First published, November 1960
Published with index, April 2014

First published by the Hatfield Branch of the
Workers' Educational Association 1960

Published with index by Hatfield Local History Society 2014

Printed on demand via www.lulu.com

Original text – copyright © 1960 Hatfield Branch of the
Workers' Educational Association (W.E.A.)

Index – copyright © 2014 Hazel K. Bell

Original text by Dr. Kenneth Hutton
Line drawings by Barbara Hutton
Photographs from various sources
Index by Hazel K. Bell
Cover design by David H. Spence

This reprint was prepared by members of Hatfield Local History Society
with the kind permission of the Workers' Educational Association.

ISBN 978-0-9928415-4-6

COVER DESIGN

Top: Hatfield and The North road sign

Bottom: The "Flying Scotsman" hauled by L.N.E.R. A.1 class
         locomotive no. 4472

FOREWORD

WHEN this series of booklets was published 50 years ago, it was rightly regarded as an exceptionally authoritative and informative work. It has since remained unchallenged as the prime source of reference for anyone interested in the history of Hatfield. Recognising its enduring value, members of Hatfield Local History Society have undertaken this reissue.

Since the booklets first appeared, some of the information contained in them has inevitably become out of date. Hatfield has been affected by sweeping changes, not least by the departure of the aircraft industry and the establishment in its place of a flourishing university and business park. Nevertheless, the original series has stood the test of time remarkably well. We know from our own research experience that it remains immensely useful and we have decided against attempting any piecemeal revision. Instead we have thought it better to reproduce the original booklets without making any changes, except for correcting obviously unintended typographical errors. An important difference is that much more comprehensive indexes have been added.

We hope that the reappearance of the work will stimulate others to undertake new research into Hatfield's more recent past.

Amongst the team who have undertaken the reissue is Henry W. Gray, M.V.O., one of the authors who took part in the W.E.A. class, led by the late Lionel Munby, which produced the original series. The others are Christine Martindale and Jane Teather, Chairman and Publications Officer respectively of Hatfield Local History Society, Hazel K. Bell, who created the new comprehensive indexes, Robin Harcourt Williams, formerly Librarian and Archivist to the Marquess of Salisbury, and G. Philip Marris who led the project.

Thanks are due to Mill Green Museum for allowing some of the original photographs to be re-scanned.

The *Workers' Educational Association,* founded in 1903, is a charity and the UK's largest voluntary sector provider of adult education, delivering 9,500 part-time courses for over 74,000 people each year in England and Scotland.

Hatfield Local History Society is an association of people interested in the history of Hatfield. The Society's aims and objectives are to encourage and undertake research into Hatfield's history, to produce publications and to provide a forum for the exchange of information on the history of the Hatfield area.

The Society is grateful to the copyright owners, the Hatfield Branch of the Workers' Educational Association, for permission to reissue the *Hatfield and its People* series. The complete list of titles is as follows:

Please contact Hatfield Local History Society for further information about this publication.

INTRODUCTION

THESE booklets represent the work over a number of years of a group of Hatfield inhabitants in a tutorial class run by the Hatfield Branch of the Workers' Educational Association under the tuition of Lionel Munby, M.A., Staff Tutor of the Extra Mural Board of Cambridge University. They are: Mrs. G. M. Brown, Mrs. N. Brown, Mrs. S. H. Dawson, Mr. W. H. Dunwoodie, Mr. H. W. Gray, Mrs. B. Hutton, Dr. K. Hutton, Mrs. M. Malcolm, Mr. W. Malcolm, Mr. T. L. Padget, Mr. M. A. Pinhorn, Mr. J. A. Preston, Mr. D. H. Spence.

I am most grateful for Mr. Munby's help and advice, and also for the co-operation of a large number of people including Col. le Hardy, of the Hertfordshire County Record Office, Lord Salisbury and the Rector of Hatfield for access to archives, the Librarian of the County Library and its branches at Hatfield and at Welwyn Garden City, the Librarians of St. Albans City Library and of Hatfield Technical College, Miss Joyce Conyngham Greene, Mr. A. G. Dixon (Stationmaster at Hatfield), and others who have kindly allowed their brains to be picked. The help of Mr. C. R. Clinker has enabled me to avoid many errors.

The chief sources of information for this booklet naturally include some books, magazines and timetables, as well as unpublished manuscripts:

a) British Transport Commission Archives at Royal Oak, W.10, for Engineers' Reports and Directors' Minutes of the G.N.R. and documents of the St. Albans branch.

b) "The Great Northern Railway" by O. S. Nock (Ian Allan, 1958).

c) "The History of the Great Northern Railway" by Charles H. Grinling (Methuen, 1898).

d) "The Railway Magazine" especially 1908 pp. 338-41 and 392-7; 1946 p. 276.

e) "Bradshaw's Railway Guide" (old copies in British Museum, and in my possession).

f) Register of Baptisms in the 17th Century (Hatfield Parish Church).

g) Turnpike Trust documents and Militia Rolls (County Record Office).

h) Great North Road documents of 1827 in the possession of Mrs. Scarborough (from the late Mr. S. C. Hankin).

i) Miscellaneous Papers in the archives of Lord Salisbury.

j) *Hertfordshire Mercury* (County Record Office).

k) *Illustrated London News* 1850 (Hatfield School Library).

l) Daniel Defoe "Tour through England and Wales" 1726.

The maps and diagrams have all been drawn specially by Mrs. Barbara Hutton and the cover by Mr. David Spence.

I hope that anyone else who has helped me will hereby accept my thanks, and that anyone who can correct or add to the information in the book will be so kind as to write to tell me.—K.H.

Published by the Hatfield Branch of the Workers' Educational Association

3

COMMUNICATIONS THROUGH HATFIELD

IN the heart of London, the road-signs point to "A1, HATFIELD AND THE NORTH" (see cover).

"On the 15th July, 1946, the 7-5 p.m. King's Cross to Aberdeen train left the track at Hatfield and crashed . . ."

"Early this morning, the Duke of Edinburgh arrived at Hatfield aerodrome and left by Comet for Ghana."

Hatfield is thus closely connected with many forms of transport, and indeed has always been so throughout its history as earlier books in this series (especially Book 1 and Book 3) have shown. The amount and type of transport has depended both on the importance of through traffic and on the size of the town itself, whilst the growth of the town is related to its communications.

THE GROWTH OF HATFIELD

By 1965, the original Parish of Hatfield (as defined in Book 1, p. 6) is likely to contain about 60,000 people, with about 25,000 of these in the 2340 acres of Hatfield New Town, and most of the others in Welwyn Garden City.

In 1948, when the New Towns Act was passed, there were about 30,000 people with 9,000 of these in what was to be the designated area of Hatfield Town, 17,000 in Welwyn Garden City, and another 4,000 in the remainder of the Parish.

In 1921, before the Garden City had started growing, there were only 5,054 inhabitants; and at the first census in 1801, 120 years previously, there were 2,442. This pattern of growth is in strong contrast with that of the rest of England and Wales which increased mostly in the 19th century, as the following table makes clear:

Population	1801	1921	1948	1965
England and Wales ...	9 million	38 million	43 million	48 million?
(increase)		*(4-fold)*	*(10%)*	*(10%)*
Hatfield and W.G.C. ...	2,442	5,054	30,000	60,000?
(increase)		*(2-fold)*	*(6-fold)*	*(2-fold)*
Hatfield (New Town Area)	(2,000)	(4,500)	9,000	25,000?
(increase)		*(2-fold)*	*(2-fold)*	*(3-fold)*

Before censuses were taken, we can only give estimates:
(a) Domesday Book, 1086: Hatfield about 300 (England 2 million);
(b) Surveys in 1221—1251: Hatfield about 600 (122—129 tenants listed);
(c) Black Death, 1349: probably about ⅓ to ½ the population died, as elsewhere;
(d) Hearth Tax, 1663 : about 1200 persons (233 households, 840 hearths);
(e) Births, 1700: about 1400 persons (1526 baptisms from 1683—1712);
(f) Militia Roll, 1758: about 2000 persons (413 men aged 18—50).

The figures from 1700 are plotted as a graph in Fig. 1 comparing the population of Hatfield with one four-thousandth of that of England and Wales. This shows even more clearly three separate stages: (a) up to 1831 when Hatfield grew at the same rate as the country as a whole; (b) from 1831 to 1921 when Hatfield stagnated; (c) from 1921 onwards, including especially the years after 1951, when Hatfield grew rapidly quite unlike the country as a whole. It is somewhat surprising to notice that the arrival of the railway in 1850 did *not* bring any notable increase in population, especially as the building of Newtown (on the site of White Lion Square, etc., see Book 1, p. 7) took place then; frankly, I find this difficult to explain.

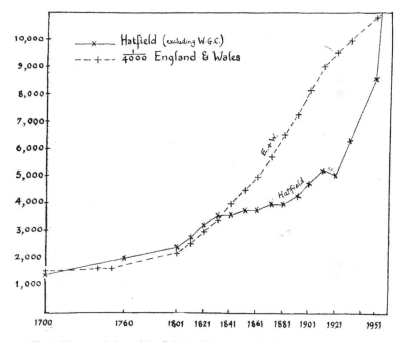

Fig. 1 The population of Hatfield Parish compared with the national growth.

ROADS THROUGH HATFIELD

If you draw a straight line from London to York as the Great Northern Railway tried to do, it goes through Hatfield. Surprisingly enough, the Romans did not do this, preferring to route Ermine Street along the Lea Valley to Ware (A.10) and thence to Royston and Huntingdon (A.14); although, as described in Book 1 p. 25, Mr. R. H. Reid has found traces of a Roman Road going past Hatfield Old Town on the east side. But apart from this "mistake" by the Romans, Hatfield has always been on some important routes from London to the North.

Even in the 13th Century, tenants of Hatfield had to perform carrying services by transporting food and goods for their Lord the Bishop of Ely from London in the South and to Kelshall (near present-day Baldock) in the North.

From very early times there may have been a route N.W. up the River Lea towards Wheathampstead (the line of the branch railway to Luton) and another route S.W. down the River Colne towards Harefield in Middlesex (near the line of the North Orbital Road); these are shown, together with Roman roads in Book 1, p. 25. More certain are the roads leading west to St. Albans and east to Hertford. The 1700 map in the frontispiece to Chauncy's "History of Hertfordshire" shows the road to St. Albans from the old town up French Horn Lane, and the road to Hertford via Park Street and Mill Green.

THE GREAT NORTH ROAD (see Fig. 15, p. 32)

The differing routes taken by the North Road through Hatfield have already been shown on maps in Book 1 (pp. 6, 8, 9, 13) but even in the 17th Century the name "Great" was applied to it. A certificate sent by some Justices of the Peace on behalf of the parishioners of Welwyn (5 miles further N.) on 28th April, 1663, states that the cost of the repair of the church was too great for them to bear unaided, and requested the Lord Chancellor, Edward Earl of Clarendon, to grant "Letters Patent under the Great Seal of England for some collection to be made on their behalf in and through such counties of this realm as your Lordship shall think fit" more especially as "the Parish is seated on the *Great Northern Road* from London and is often a place of worship for many persons travelling that road who rest there on Sabbath days".

Among those who travelled at that time was, of course, Samuel Pepys, whose account of Hatfield's Inns has been mentioned in Book 3 (p. 28), who gives some idea of the discomforts of travel. In October, 1664, he "got by night to Stevenage, and there mighty merry, though I in bed more weary than the other two days, which, I think, proceeded from our galloping so much". The next day, "it raining, we set out, and about nine o'clock got to Hatfield in church time, . . . to Barnet by the end of sermon, and there dined at the Red Lyon very weary again, but all my weariness yesterday night and today in my thighs only". In September, 1663, Pepys's wife was with him and the journey from Brampton to London was too much for her: at Biggleswade, "up very betimes by break of day, and got my wife up, whom the thought of this day's journey do discourage; and after eating something . . . we mounted, and through Baldwicke (Baldock) . . . and so to Hatfield, it being most curious weather from the time we set out to our getting home, and here we dined, and my wife being very weary, and believing that it would be hard to get her home tonight, and a great charge to keep her longer abroad, I took the opportunity of an empty coach that

6

was to go to London, and left her to come in it to London, for half-a-crown". (Don't think that Pepys was an old man; he was only 30 at the time, and his wife probably younger.)

But what kind of road was the Great North Road when first it came into favour? W. Branch Johnson in "Welwyn, Briefly" (1960) says: "Since for centuries it had been used almost exclusively by horse and foot traffic, it was soft surfaced, rutted, pot-holed and undrained, dust-laden and dung-covered in dry weather, deep in mire and dung as soon as rain fell. For literally hundreds of years . . . landholders had been in trouble for allowing trees and hedges to overgrow and impede it, for building out-houses that jutted into it, for digging chalkpits that under-mined it. Such repair as it received was left to tenants of the manor, . . . unwilling householders being compelled to work for six days a year on road repair . . ." What happens when the maintenance of a road is left to the private enterprise of parishioners or frontagers is vividly illustrated by a visit to present-day Cuffley; almost any of the private roads, especially those near the school, will puncture your cycle tyres, break your car springs, spatter you with mud, and bring you into a thoroughly 17th century frame of mind about the "ease of travel".

In the 18th century, the barley of North Hertfordshire and of East Anglia for Londoners' beer, was brought from Royston to Ware in waggons drawn by strings of up to fifty pack-horses, before thankfully being transferred to barges on the River Lea. No wonder that the coaches preferred the north road through Hatfield, but even it was in very bad condition in 1726: "There is a road which is a branch of the northern road, and is properly called the coach road; . . . and this indeed is a most frightful way if we take it from Hatfield or rather from the Park corner of Hatfield House, and from then to Stevenage to Baldock, Biggleswade and Bugden. Here is that famous lane called Baldock Lane, famous for being so impassable that the coaches and travellers were obliged to break out of the way even by force, which the people of this country not able to prevent it then placed gates and laid open their lands, setting men at the gates to take voluntary toll which travellers always chose to pay rather than plunge into the sloughs and holes that no horse could wade through". (Daniel Defoe)

Soon after this, in 1730, the Galley Corner Turnpike Trust was formed, which took over the responsibility for maintaining the road from Galley Corner in Middlesex (near Barnet) to Lemsford Mill in the north of Hatfield parish. A tollgate was set up near Jack Oldings to collect the tolls for the trust. The toll-house still exists (Fig. 2, p. 8) on the east side of A.1000 just north of the North Orbital Road.

This was a great improvement on the previous system by which the parish was responsible for the upkeep of all roads running through it, both local and through roads, and had to raise the money from the rates.

In 1783 the Trust diverted the road from the route shown in Book 1 (pp. 11—12): "April 21st.—This is to give notice that by order of the Commissioners of the Galley Corner Turnpike, the new Road from

Woodside Green thro Milwards Park to Hatfield will be opened for public use on Thursday 1st May next, on which day the old road will be shut up. Richard Edmonds, surveyor."

Fig. 2   Toll house on the old Great North Road (p. 7)

It is said that a route for the Great North Road was surveyed by Telford for the Trust, but the project of building a road to Telford's specification was too expensive and was abandoned.

In some cases where many cattle were driven to market a Drove Road was used in order to take the animals a way that avoided the toll-gates. It may be that the Green Lanes—Travellers Lane route is such a drove road to avoid the Hatfield Tolls, as it has the reputation locally of being a way to London. This route leaves the main-road at Lemsford Church and goes by Green Lanes, Briars Lane, Travellers Lane and Marshmoor Lane to Bell Bar, where it may have gone on to join the "way from Hertford to London thro' the Green Lanes", which ran from Camfield Farm to Dolamores Pot Bar, and so finally to the Boar and Castle in Oxford Street, by way of Smithfield and Holborn.

One can well imagine that in the old coaching days Fore Street was a very considerable thoroughfare and it would have been quite a common sight to see the coaches struggling up the steep hill or carefully making their way downwards. Understandably there are many stories of those days. James the 2nd Marquis of Salisbury is said to have experimented with wood block paving in Fore Street: apparently he was a pioneer of this method of road surfacing. On one occasion the York Waggon is said to have needed no less than 16 horses to climb the hill. At one time as many as 70 coaches used Hatfield and it is therefore

8

not surprising to learn that hostelries were plentiful; there were at least 14 in Fore Street and Back Street at one time or another, the sites of which are marked in Book 3 (Fig. 2, p. 8).

The end of the 18th and early 19th centuries were the heyday of the old Great North Road, with wagons and coaches passing in great numbers through Hatfield every day. In Hatfield lived the man, Joseph Scarborough, who from 1830 was responsible for the carriers' wagon service between Hatfield and Baldock, along this road. He undertook "to work the common stage waggons called Messrs. Jackson and Co., Leeds and London Waggons, between Hatfield and Baldock down one day and back the next day; every day down and up alternately day for day in the time specified in the printed Time Bill now in use, viz.: in 7 hours and 12 minutes, the distance being 18 miles and I hereby further engage that if I do not work the such waggon (whether it be a 6-inch or a 9-inch wheeled waggon with cart attached) in the time stated to the satisfaction of the parties concerned I will relinquish the same and all concern and interest therein on receiving a notice of one calendar month if such notice be signed by two-thirds of the other parties working the said waggons. As witness my hand this 22nd day of June 1830—(signed) Joseph Scarborough." The distance was then estimated as 18 miles, but in 1835 the whole road from Leeds to London was surveyed and measured, and "Mr. Scarboro's Stage" came to only 17 miles 0 furlongs and 179¾ yards, though this was after the "New Road" was built from Stanborough to Brickwall Hill, which saved 418 yards. Joseph Scarborough also owned the Eight Bells Inn, which he bought from Nathaniel Cheek in 1827 with "all Fixtures Household Furniture Stock in trade etc. at a fare Valuation".

The accounts of the Galley Corner Turnpike show that all this careful measuring led to increased revenue. The income from tolls which had amounted to £1800 in 1812 had fallen steadily year by year to £1306 8s. 2d. in 1826-7 and just £1000 in 1834. In 1835 they had risen to £1460 and by 1839 were at an "all-time-high" with £1880. Thereafter tolls fell steadily to £1000 in 1848, £500 in 1852, and £250 in 1862.

The road was altered to its present course (A.1000) by special Act of Parliament at the time the Railway was built in 1850. Lord Salisbury agreed to let the Railway come through Hatfield on condition that a station was built convenient to his house, and he built a new approach by the viaduct crossing over Park Street from the station to the north door of Hatfield House which now became the front door.

THE COMING OF THE RAILWAY

The railways have always made most of their money by carrying goods, not passengers, and so the first railways were those joining important commercial centres, Stockton and Darlington (1825), Liverpool and Manchester (1830), London and Birmingham (1838). The latter line went through Watford, and by 1842 there was a line up the valley of the Lea through Broxbourne as far as Bishops Stortford (Fig. 3, p. 10). But

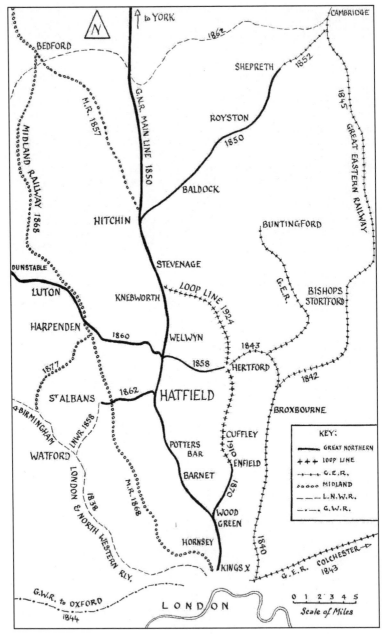

Fig. 3   Railways from London to the North

10

there was no line directly to the North. A line had in fact been promoted in 1824 to pass through Hatfield (the London and Northern Railroad, surveyed by George Stephenson) but was not proceeded with because there was no immediate traffic to be expected.

On 3rd May, 1844, however, the first prospectus of the "London and York" railway was issued, stating that "the line of railway should commence at London, near King's Cross, and proceed in the direction of Barnet, Hatfield, Hitchin, Biggleswade, St. Neots and Huntingdon to Peterborough", and thence to York. The next prospectus a month later explained that the two main objects of the undertaking were to shorten the distance between London and the northern parts of the Kingdom, i.e. by using the most direct route in spite of any difficulties (Fig. 4, p. 11) and to connect a population of one and a half million in Yorkshire with a population in London of about equal amount (and especially to transport coal from Yorkshire, Derbyshire and Nottinghamshire to London).

The rector of Hatfield, Rev. F. J. Faithfull, gave evidence on 10th May, 1845, in favour of the proposed railway to the parliamentary committee, saying that "The scarcity of coal had an unfavourable effect on the inhabitants' morals. It drove them from their desolate homes to seek comfort in public houses and other places of questionable resort".

Another very important point was that this line had "the hearty concurrence and support" of the landowners affected. That is a polite way of saying that so fiercely had Lord Dacre of Codicote objected to the line going via Welwyn and Codicote to Hitchin (like the A.600 road), that it was necessary to build the vast Welwyn Viaduct (Fig. 12) over the River Mimram. Even in 1960 when at last there

Fig. 4   Great Northern
to the North

11

is quadruple track all the way to Welwyn Garden City, the 102 ft. deep valley (500 yards wide) of the little Mimram prevents its extension to Hitchin. Lord Salisbury, by comparison, was fairly welcoming to the railway, and took the opportunity to divert the Great North Road from inside his park to run alongside the railway (Book 1, pp. 8-9), the G.N.R. paying £8,000 towards the cost of the deviation.

THE CONSTRUCTION OF THE MAIN LINE

In the parliamentary session of 1845-6 at the height of the "railway mania" no fewer than 815 Railway Bills awaited consideration. The London and York Bill (incorporating the Great Northern Railway Company) had to contend with fierce opposition (which cost it £251,144), but at last it received the Royal Assent on 26th June, 1846, the same date as Sir Robert Peel's bill to Repeal the Corn Laws.

Actual construction began in August, 1847, and the monthly manuscript reports of the Chief Engineer, Joseph Cubitt, can be seen at the British Transport Commission's Archives. The first 14 miles out of London, rising steeply at a gradient of 1 in 200 throughout to beyond Potters Bar, was by far the most difficult, with its seven tunnels (Fig. 5) and its sticky clay which rendered work almost impossible in the winter months. By contrast, the next 30 miles of the "Hitchin District" through Hatfield was mostly gravel or chalk country and far easier to work. The total number of men employed in constructing the "200 miles" of line average about 8,000, with "957 men and 193 horses for the month of August, 1848" being the largest number in the Hitchin District. Lord Salisbury found out on 13th April, 1847, that "Mr. Brassey does not anticipate more than 250 men being located sufficiently near to Hatfield to take up their quarters there. They may be detained about 18 months. The rule is to give one policeman to 60 men, so that a superintendent and 3 men would be sufficient". We do not know where the men did live, but there is a record of a quarrel between railway labourers in the Eight Bells in 1850 (see Book 3, p. 18).

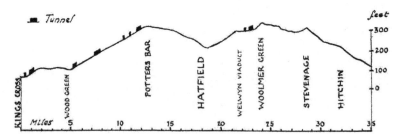

Fig. 5   The steep climb out of London

12

At Bell Bar, in September, 1848, the G.N.R. was operating its own brickmaking works for bridges, etc. The men were paid in vouchers exchangeable for goods at the employer's shop in spite of the provisions of the Truck Act, and the employer got a 10% rake off.

The famous "Hunters Bridge" at Welwyn Garden City, which until reconstruction in 1960 was a notorious bottleneck, and which used to divide the town into "west-side boss-class" and "east-side working-class", is mentioned on 1st June, 1848. "The cutting at Hatfield, No. 10, is also stopped in consequence of a Bridge having been required without sufficient notice being given." (Hatfield Parish Boundary then lay along what is now the north side of the Campus; see Book 1, p. 6.)

By 13th February, 1850, "the formation of the line is completed except the additional excavation for the station at Hatfield"; and on Wednesday, 7th August, 1850 (not the 8th as often stated), the Great Northern Railway was opened from London (through Hatfield) to Peterborough, and described in the *Illustrated London News* of that week. This paper in its "Chronology of Remarkable Events for the half year" also records: "September 21. Collision at the Hatfield Station, Great Northern Railway; seven persons seriously injured.—A boy, aged twelve years, died at Cheltenham from excessive smoking."

HATFIELD IN 1850

The Hatfield of 1850, to which the railway came, was a small and not particularly healthy or pleasant place by present-day standards. Miscellaneous papers at Hatfield House have records of a Famine Fast in 1847, Smallpox in 1848, and Cholera in 1849. S. Lewis's "Topographical Directory" of 1849 says of Hatfield: "The town consist of one principal street intersected by a smaller one, both of which during the winter months lighted by oil. A silk mill worked by a steam engine furnishes employment to about 200 persons, chiefly children; and there is a paper mill on the river. The great railway from London to York will pass by the town. A court leet is held by the Marquis of Salisbury as Lord of the Manor. There is a school of industry for girls, with an endowment given in 1733 by Anne, Countess of Salisbury; and almshouses for widows founded and endowed by the families of Boteler and Salisbury."

Even Rev. F. J. Faithfull's hopes (p. 11) do not seem to have materialized, because Book 3 records the first mention of eight new pubs in 1850 or 1851: Black Bull, Compasses, Great Northern, Green Man, Gun, Jacob's Well, Robin Hood, White Lion. But the prominence given to the church in the picture (Fig. 6, which presumably dates from about this time), is no accident; the 1851 census recorded that out of 3,862 persons, no fewer than 1,274 attended adult services at church or chapel. (This compares with about 1,350 adults in 1959 out of a population of 18,000.)

There were eight trains per day out of London in 1850, all going as far as Hitchin, and *all* stopping at Hatfield, even including the 7-40

Fig. 6   Hatfield from the Line (about 1860?)

a.m. Scotch Express which reached Hatfield (first stop) at 8-12 a.m., and York (via Boston and Lincoln) at 2-50 p.m. (In 1873, there were 19 trains per day from London to Hatfield; in 1960, 62 trains.)

The effect of the railway on the inhabitants of Hatfield is not recorded, but the *Illustrated London News* of 21/9/1850 commented in an editorial "The Great lines of railway in England, by granting facilities for 'monster' or excursion trains at cheap rates have conferred a boon upon the public and have increased, let us hope, the dividends of their shareholders". For example, in the last five days of February, 1856, according to *The Times,* 21,843½ passengers were booked from Peter-borough to London (76 miles) at a fare of one shilling (2nd class)! According to the population statistics (Fig. 1, p. 5), the railway seems to have encouraged the people of Hatfield parish to *leave* the district, probably for London, whence they are returning as citizens of the New Town in 1951-1965.

Nevertheless, many old or new inhabitants of Hatfield Town were employed by the railway, either as station staff, at the signal boxes, in the engineering department, and particularly in the locomotive depot which is still a characteristic (and sooty) feature of the Hatfield scene. Probably about 120 in all were employed, and probably many lived in the Newtown area ("Rights of Way", etc.) just then being built, and just now being demolished.

The labour force of 250 (mainly Irish) engaged in construction did *not* remain in Hatfield, because it was a few years before the branch lines were constructed, and the most noticeable result of the railway was its effect on the landscape.

BRIDGES AND LEVEL CROSSINGS

Those of us who think of Hatfield as a "traffic island" cut off from the surrounding countryside by streams of dangerously fast-moving traffic, will sympathise with the people of Hatfield in the 1850's who found themselves cut off from work or from friends by the line of the new railway. Quite clearly the Great North Road (A.1000) was too important to rely on a level crossing, and the "wiggle" by the Wrestlers Inn diverted the road over the railway at not too acute an angle (Book 1, p. 8, top). But on 19/11/1852 "the recent very large amount of rain has put the Permanent Way considerably out of order. The principal casualty has been a slip in a place where one would be least likely to expect such an occurrence, viz. in a gravel cutting at Hatfield, which slip extending beneath the abutment of the Great North Turnpike Road Bridge brought a portion of the abutment and part of two of the arches down".

The very long footbridge just south of Hatfield Station was the cause of much ill-feeling in 1861 when the G.N.R. made it all 7 feet higher so that the "chimneys of engines could pass underneath on the near side". The Parish Council protested, and the 2nd Marquis of Salisbury himself wrote (on House of Lords notepaper) to say . . . "I imagine that the Parish will not submit to the invasion which the G.N. Company has made upon their rights of road without taking some steps upon the subject and I must say that they will be fully justified in doing so". The trouble was that the bridge could no longer be approached by a ramp, but had to have steps (as it does now). But the company took legal advice: "we are not aware of any obligation by which Railway Companies are required to construct Bridges of this kind in a particular form, or to make them available for wheeling Barrows or other things over them . . . and we consider it is not expedient to concur in the suggestion of the Marquis of Salisbury to submit the question to the decision of a Vestry Meeting." So Hatfield citizens lost Round 1.

Round 2 concerned the level crossing by which the St. Albans Road originally crossed the railway direct from School Lane to the Red Lion (Book 1, Fig. 4). Only one year later, on 8th March, 1862, the promoters of the Hatfield and St. Albans Railway (with ⅓ of the capital subscribed by the G.N.R.) wanted to buy some of Lord Salisbury's land, but the Marquis insisted, according to his solicitor's letter:

(1) The Level Road accross *(sic)* the Great Northern Line to be diverted and carried over the Great Northern Line by a Bridge—this a *sine quâ non.*

(2) £500 an acre for the land in Hatfield Parish.

(3) £200 an acre for other land.

(4) Liberty to drain into the company's drain.

(5) Solicitors costs to be paid.

15

A week later another snorter arrived at the G.N.R. offices from the Board of Trade (Railway Dept.): "I am directed by the Lords of Committee of the Privy Council for Trade to remind you of the letter from this Dept. of 21 February, and the Memorial signed by the Rector and other inhabitants of Hatfield relative to the Level Crossing by the Great Northern Railway of the High Road leading from Hertford and Hatfield to St. Albans . . ."

Although an agreement about the bridge was signed in 1862, it was still necessary to remind the Hatfield and St. Albans Railway on 15/4/1864 that "the right is reserved to Lord Salisbury to retain possession of the whole of his land until the bridge is built in accordance with an agreed plan." The G.N.R. directors realized that "they would save £120 per year on wages and expenses at the Level Crossing and also acquire the signalman's cottage", and so the citizens of Hatfield thus won Round 2, and had a proper bridge.

Three other level crossings were done away with in 1879 as a condition of the Board of Trade giving permission for the use of a third line between Hatfield and Potters Bar for up slow trains instead of only for goods. The crossing immediately south of Howe Dell was replaced by the present road bridge on higher ground by which Oxlease Drive joins Briars Lane to the A.1000 North Road. Just south of the Parish boundary, the crossing of Travellers Lane over the line near Marshmoor (see Fig. 7) was done away with by extending the road along the west side of the railway to the Welham Green bridge. And thirdly the present rather awkwardly shaped bridge by Brookmans Park station replaced a level crossing which crossed the line diagonally.

Evidently it took considerable pressure in the nineteenth century, as in the twentieth, to persuade powerful corporations to provide members of the public with a means of crossing traffic arteries in safety.

BRANCH LINES

THE HERTFORD BRANCH. A month after the opening of the railway to Hatfield, "the inhabitants of Hertford and of Hatfield have memorialized the G.N.R. to construct the railway between those points, for which they already have parliamentary sanction" (I.L.N. 21/9/50), but in November of that year, Lord Salisbury wrote to the Mayor of Hertford opposing such a railway because of the detriment to his property, and declining to receive a deputation (and in fact the G.N.R. did *not* have parliamentary sanction). This may explain the curious route which was eventually adopted, namely for three miles north alongside the G.N.R. to just beyond where W.G.C. Station now stands, and then south-eastwards via Cole Green and Hertingfordbury to Hertford (North) (see Fig. 7). The line was opened on 1st March, 1858, by a separate company (the Hertford and Welwyn Junction Railway, incorporated 3/7/1854) which amalgamated on 28th June, 1858, with the Welwyn—Luton railway, and then with the G.N.R. in 1861. There was a connection at Hertford with the Great Eastern line.

16

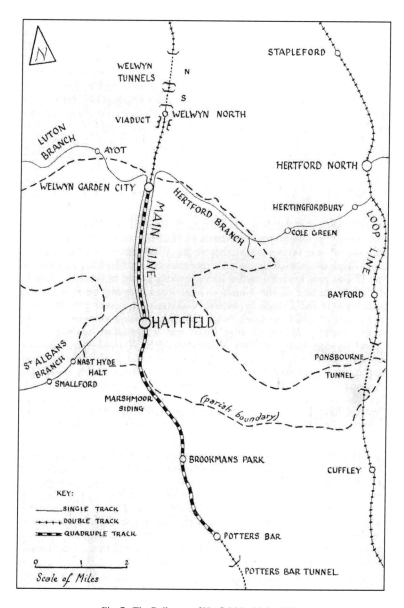

Fig. 7   The Railways of Hatfield Parish in 1950

17

THE LUTON AND DUNSTABLE BRANCH. The Luton, Dunstable and Welwyn Co. was incorporated on 16th July, 1855, and by 3rd May, 1858 passenger trains ran from Dunstable to Luton, but not till 1st September, 1860, was the whole branch line in operation up to Welwyn Junction, where passengers seem to have alighted at the side of the line. By October, 1860, Hatfield had become a proper railway junction, and the trains both to Hertford and to Luton and Dunstable departed from it—instead of from the middle of the Welwyn countryside. Luton and Harpenden thus had their rail links to London via the G.N. line before the Midland Railway was extended southwards from Bedford. Luton's chief industry at that time was straw hat-making, to which many Hatfield inhabitants contributed straw-plait (Book 2, p. 30). The importance of this line even today (the only one of Hatfield's three branches still carrying passenger traffic) can be seen from the trains of huge wooden crates labelled "General Motors, Valparaiso", "General Motors, Melbourne", taking Vauxhall Bedford trucks from Luton to the ends of the earth, via Hatfield.

ST. ALBANS BRANCH. The route from Hatfield to St. Albans, now mostly of interest to inhabitants of Hatfield, was for eight years of vital importance to the inhabitants of St. Albans because a coach along it provided them with a rail link to London, via Hatfield, and before that it was part of a Turnpike Road leading as far as Reading. Traces of this forerunner of the North Orbital Road can still be seen on the milestones at the Comet or outside Oaklands; it would puzzle many present-day motorists to work out a route for those 49 miles to Reading. In the Railway Mania of 1845 there was a grandiose scheme for a Round-London Railway from Slough through Watford—St. Albans—Hatfield—Hertford. The trouble started when the L.N.W. built their branch from Watford to St. Albans in 1858. In October 1861, Mr. Seymour Clarke, General Manager of the G.N.R. reported to his directors that "we used to have ⅔ of the St. Albans to London traffic but now we have lost it all to the new L.N.W. branch. It is vital for us to have a branch line to St. Albans and a separate station there."

In 1862 the "Hatfield and St. Albans Railway Co." was formed. In 1863 a new competitor appeared when the Midland Railway obtained powers to extend their line from Bedford through Luton and St. Albans to London, instead of via Hitchin and the G.N. main line (Fig. 3, p. 10). In spite of this threat, the little five mile branch line was opened on 16th October, 1865—but by 17th July, 1866, an Extraordinary General Meeting was held proposing to transfer it to the G.N.R. because it couldn't make ends meet. It did, in fact, survive as an independent company (whose Minutes, Ledger, Day Book, etc., are still in existence) until absorbed by the G.N.R. on 1st November, 1883.

It is interesting to note that, by the agreement of 1862, the "G.N.R. shall, at the request of the Hatfield and St. Albans Railway Company, yield and deliver up the said railway stations (Smallford, etc.) and works in a state of good repair" in the year A.D. 2861! The most unusual feature of the branch was its three special ORCHID VANS belonging to Messrs. Sanders labelled "to be returned to St. Albans" but in fact often used for carrying straw hats from Luton to London. Although there were many passengers, especially on market days after Hatfield's market had ceased in 1873, one of the chief sources of revenue seems to have been transporting the Salvation Army's *War Cry* from the Campfield Printing Works at St. Albans all over the world.

SUBURBAN TRAFFIC

On 6th December, 1849, the engineer recommended building "stations at Barnet (9¾ miles), Hatfield (17½ miles) and Welwyn (22 miles), and probably also one at Potters Bar (12½ miles)". There was, of course, no proper station at Welwyn Garden City until 5th October, 1926, though the "Halt" opened in 1920 merited a cartoon in *Punch* (Fig. 8). The station at Brookmans Park was also opened in 1926 (19th July). Finsbury Park station only began (as "Seven Sisters Road") in 1861, but there were stations at Hornsey and at Colney Hatch (Southgate) earlier on, as will be seen from the following letter, dated 18th April, 1857, "signed by upwards of 110 Season Ticket Holders and other constant Travellers on the line, who in the aggregate represent an income of about £1500 a year to the company" asking the directors of the G.N.R. "for a train to be run from Kings Cross to Hatfield on a Saturday afternoon about 3 p.m.

"We . . . beg most respectfully to request your co-operation and assistance with a view to give effect to the present movement in favour of a Saturday half holiday.

"It seems pretty generally agreed that the time of closing offices and places of business should be two o'clock on Saturday and our desire is that the benefits of Railway Communication should be fully extended to those persons who will thus get released from business at an early hour on Saturday.

"At present there is no train from Kings Cross between 1-55 and 4 o'clock p.m. and we would suggest for your kind consideration . . . the postponing of the former of those two trains till about 3 o'clock or . . . that a short train should be dispatched at about that hour on Saturdays only . . ."

The only addresses that *might* be Hatfield on that list (the general standard of handwriting strikes me as appalling) were Jno. Cater, A. Cater and Jno. Jas. Cater; most of the signatories lived in Hornsey or Barnet. It is pleasant to record that the secretary minuted "the train to be tried for the summer", by "one of the Coal Engines, which will take up its load of empties for the return journey at Hatfield and north thereof". In the 1873 "Bradshaw", there were two "Saturdays only" trains on the line, namely the 2-19 p.m. to Barnet, and the 3-3 p.m. to Wood Green, which both returned to King's Cross. Evidently there were not enough "commuters" from Potters Bar or Hatfield to warrant running these trains so far. (Fig. 9, p. 22).

19

By 1924, however, enough Welwyn Garden Citizens travelled each day from their platform in mid-mud (on the west side of the Luton branch line) to warrant a full-page cartoon in *Punch* (Fig. 8).

[Reproduced by kind permission of "Punch"

Fig. 8.

RAILWAY TRAVEL IN LATE VICTORIAN TIMES

From Bradshaw's Guide for 1873 (Fig. 9) it is clear that the railway service was still developing fast. There were for some years also through trains from Herne Hill on the Chatham line to Hatfield, and North London Railway trains from Broad Street in addition. By 1887, although trains were not as comfortable or as frequent as today, they were as *fast* as at any time in the following seventy years before the introductions of the diesels in 1959 (and electrification in 1963?).

Hatfield was an important town on the Great Northern Railway, in many ways more important than it is now. There were, of course, no cars and no buses; but the 9-05 a.m. train from King's Cross which arrived in Hatfield at 9-49 a.m. "ran forward to Welwyn, Knebworth, Stevenage or Hitchin when required to convey *Hunting Gentlemen with Horses*".

Hatfield was connected not merely with King's Cross, with Hitchin, and with Luton (as now), but also with St. Albans and with Hertford. As a Junction, Hatfield was therefore entitled to a Refreshment Room (opened in about 1879)—which it still has—unlike the new station at Welwyn Garden City whose citizens consider their town superior to Hatfield in every other respect, and resent this mark of its unimportance.

Nowadays, in our march towards a classless society, we not merely have trains of one class only, but recently (1956) third class passengers were all converted into second class at one stroke of the pen. Not so in 1887; then there really were three classes ("King's Cross to Hatfield, Fare 2/6 1st class, 1/10 2nd class, 1/5½ 3rd class"). Moreover the 10-30 p.m. from King's Cross "stops at Hatfield to set down (only) First Class London Passengers"—with no doubt the Third Marquis often among them. If 2nd or 3rd class passengers missed the 9-30 p.m., they had to wait till the 12-05 a.m. due in at Hatfield at 12-55 a.m. Surely this last train is the direct ancestor of the infamous 11-59 p.m. which now (in theory) takes two minutes less than 70 years ago.

From London there were, in 1887, 24 trains per day, averaging 39 minutes journey time, and the fastest train was the 11-10 a.m. which only took 26 minutes because it did not stop at Finsbury Park; this was three minutes faster than the pre-1959 record-breaker (the 10-40 a.m.), but the recently accelerated service has *just one* train (the 12-34 p.m.) which beats it by *just one* minute. (Downhill into London is two minutes faster). By 1958 the journey time averaged 42 minutes (but there were 50 trains per day), and by 1960 the average is 36 minutes for the 60 trains per day. Thus although we did not, until recently, travel faster, yet we can travel more frequently and especially more comfortably; it can have been no joke being rattled along in the four-wheelers shown in Fig. 10 (p. 24).

LONDON, BARNET, HATFIELD, ST. ALBANS, HITCHIN, &c.—Great Northern.

Down.	mrn	mrn	mrn	mrn	mrn	mrn	mrn	mrn	mrn	mrn	mrn	mrn	mrn	mrn	aft	aft	aft	aft	aft	aft	aft	aft	aft	aft
Victoria ....dep	....	....	....	....	6 28	....	8 8	8 8	8 18	9 18	9 35	1043	1055	1138	1220	1 8	1 37	....	1 47	1 47	1 47	2 37	2 48	3 2
Ludgate Hill. ,,	....	....	....	....	7 1	....	8 43	8 43	8 51	9 50	10 9	1118	1129	1221	1254	1 41	2 12	....	2 21	2 21	2 21	3 11	3 22	3 39
Moorgate St.. ,,	....	6 0	6 0	....	7 15	....	8 36	8 36	8 57	9 43	1016	....	1143	1225	1 10	1 49	1 58	2 6	2 27	2 34	2 34	....	3 32	3 32
Aldersgate St. ,,	....	6 2	6 2	....	7 17	....	8 38	8 38	8 59	9 45	1 18	....	1145	1227	1 12	1 51	2 0	2 8	2 29	2 36	2 36	....	3 34	3 34
Farringdon St ,,	....	6 4	6 4	....	7 19	....	8 46	8 40	9 1	9 54	1020	1122	1147	1229	1 14	1 53	2 16	2 10	2 31	2 38	2 38	3 14	3 36	3 48
King's C. (Met),,	....	6 8	6b8	....	7 23	....	8 50	8b44	9 5	9 58	1024	1126	1151	1233	1b18	1 57	2 20	2 14	2b35	2b42	2b42	3 18	3b40	3 47
,, (G.N.),,	5 30	6 20	6 30	7 25	7 35	8 0	8 55	9 0	9 15	10 5	1035	1135	1250	1240	1 25	2 2	2 27	2 19	2 45	3 0	3 3	3 23	3 50	3 55
Holloway	5 35	6 25		....	7 40	....	9 0		....	1010	....	1140		1245	....	2 7	2 32	2 24	....	....	3 8	3 28	....	4 0
Finsbury Park..	5 38	6 28		....	7 43	....	9 3		....	1013	....	1143		1248	....	2 10	2 35	2 27	....	....	3 11	3 31	....	4 3
Hornsey	5 43	6 33	1. Station for Alexandra Park.	7 33	7 46	....	9 8	a A carriage detached.	....	1018	....	1147	b Change carriages at King's Cross.	1252	....	2 16	2 40	2 32	....	....	3 16	3 35	....	4 8
Wood Green 1 ..	5 46	6 43		....	7 51	....	9 13		....	1021	....	1150		1255	....	2 19	2 43	2 35	....	....	3 19	3 38	....	4 11
Southgte & Colny	5 51	6 47		7 39	7 58	8 14	9 18		9 28	1026	....	1155		1 0	....	2 24	2 48	2 40	....	....		3 43	4 4	4 16
Barnet .. [Hatch	5 58	6 54		7 46	8 3	8 21	9 25		9 35	1033	1054	12 2		1 8	1 45	2 31	....	2 49	....	....		3 50	4 11	....
Potter's Bar	....	....		7 54	8 13	8 31	....		9 43	1043	11 4	....		....	1 53	2 41	....		....	3 2		....	4 21	....
Hatfld 117,118	....	....		8 6	8 23	8 43	....		9 53	1055	1120	....		....	2 4	2 52	....	Satrdys only.	a	....	Saturdays only.	....	4 34	....
118 St. Albans a	....	....		9 5	....	9 5	....	a	1015	....	12 3	....		....	....	3 28	....		3 28	....		....	....	....
Welwyn	....	....		8 15	....	8 53	....		d	....	1129	....		....	2 13	....	....		....	....		....	4 44	....
Stevenage	....	....		8 27	....	9 5	....		d	....	1141	....		....	2 25	....	....		....	....		....	4 56	....
Hitchin 118,179	....	....	7 15	8 35	8 59	9 13	....	9 45	d	....	1148	....	1245	....	2 31	....	....		....	....		....	5 4	....

Continued.	aft	aft	aft	aft	aft	aft	aft	aft	aft	aft	aft	aft	aft	aft	aft	aft	aft	Sundays.					
Victoria ....dep	3 2	3 52	3 52	4 2	4 23	4 23	4 33	5 4	5 47	6 1	6 38	7 7	7 25	7 58	8 46	9 45	1050	....	....	4 45	6 45	8 20	
Ludgate Hill. ,,	4 0	4 27	4 27	4 35	4 56	4 56	5 9	5 39	6 23	6 31	7 13	7 49	8 6	8 32	9 21	1019	1127	....	....	5 22	7 22	8 57	
Moorgate St. ,,	4 9	4 21	4 38	4 38	4 38	5 5	5 18	5 50	6 9	6 44	7 15	7 53	8 16	8 29	9 46	1044	1138	7 12	8 43	5 45	7 41	9 5	
Aldersgate St ,,	4 11	4 23	4 40	4 40	4 40	5 7	5 20	5 52	6 11	6 46	7 17	7 55	8 18	8 31	9 48	1046	1140	7 14	8 45	5 47	7 43	9 7	
Farringdon St ,,	4 13	4 31	4 42	4 42	5 0	5 9	5 22	5 54	6 27	6 48	7 19	7 57	8 20	8 36	9 50	1048	1142	7 16	8 47	5 49	7 45	9 9	
King's C. (Met),,	4b17	4 35	4b49	4b46	5 4	5b13	5 26	5 58	6 31	6 52	7 23	8 1	8b24	8 40	9 54	1052	1146	7b20	8 51	5 53	7b49	9 13	
,, (G.N) ,,	4 25	4 42	5 0	5 5	5 15	5 30	5 33	6 5	6 40	7 0	7 35	8 6	8 40	8 45	10 0	11 0	12 0	7 30	9 0	6 0	8 0	9 20	
Holloway	....	....	....	....	5 20	....	5 38	....	6 45	7 5	7 40	8 11	....	8 50	10 5	11 5	12 5	7 35	9 5	6 5	8 5	9 25	
Finsbury Park..	....	....	....	....	5 23	....	5 41	....	6 48	7 8	7 43	8 1[illegible]	....	8 53	10 8	11 8	12 8	7 39	9 9	6 8	8 9	9 29	
Hornsey	....	4 51	....	....	5 28	....	5 46	....	6 53	7 13	7 48	8 19	....	8 58	1015	1115	1215	7 46	9 17	6 15	8 14	9 35	c Change for Metropolitan Line. d Proceeds to Welwyn on Mondays, Wednesdays, and Fridays, and to Stevenage and Hitchin on Mondays.
Wood Green 1 ..	....	4 54	....	....	5 31	....	5 49	....	6 56	7 16	7 51	8 22	....	9 1	1018	1118	1218	7 50	9 23	6 18	8 19	9 40	
Southgte & Colny	....	4 59	....	....	5 36	....	5 54	6 19	7 0	7 21	7 56	8 26	....	9 5	1023	1123	1223	7 55	9 28	6 22	8 24	9 45	
Barnet.. [Hatch	....	5 6	....	5 24	....	....	6 1	6 26	7 7	7 28	8 3	8 33	....	9 12	1032	1132	1232	8 3	9 37	6 30	8 32	9 53	
Potter's Bar	....	....	....	a	....	....	....	6 36	....	7 39	8 13	....	....	9 21	1043	....	1243	8 14	9 47	6 40	8 43	10 4	
Hatfld 117,118	4 55	....	....	5 42	....	a	....	6 48	....	7 50	8 23	....	9 9	....	1055	....	1255	8 27	10 0	6 52	8 55	1015	
118 St. Albans a	5 8	....	....	6 18	....	6 18	....	....	....	....	9 24	....	9 24	....	....	....	....	8 52	....	....	....	1032	
Welwyn	....	....	....	5 50	....	....	....	6 58	....	....	8 37	....	....	....	....	....	....	8 38	1011	7 2	9 5	....	
Stevenage	....	....	....	6 1	....	....	....	7 9	....	....	8 49	....	....	....	....	....	....	8 50	1022	7 15	9 17	....	
Hitchin 118,179	5 15		d 5 45	6 8				7 16			8 59		9 29	....	....	....	....	8 58	1030	7 23	9 25	....	

Fm Cambrdge 118	mrn	mrn	mrn	mrn	mrn	mrn	mrn	mrn	mrn	mrn	mrn	mrn	mrn	mrn	mrn	mrn	mrn	mrn	aft	aft	aft	aft	aft	aft
Hitchin......dep	2 20		....	....	....	7 20	....	....	8 12	8 47	9 13	....	9 38	....	1055	....	....	1115	....	....	....	....	2 35	
Stevenage	....		....	....	....	7 28	....	....	8 20	....	....	....	9 46	....	....	....	....	1124	....	....	....	....	2 43	
Welwyn	....	Workmen's Train, 3rd cl	....	....	....	7 41	....	....	8 33	....	....	....	9 58	....	....	....	....	1136	....	....	....	....	2 55	Satrdys only.
118 St. Albans d	....		....	....	....	....	....	8 2	....	....	....	....	9 42	....	....	11 4	....	....	....	....	1 38	....	....	
Hatfield 117,118	....		....	....	7 33	7 53	....	8 26	8 47	....	....	....	1011	1025	....	1120	....	1148	....	....	1 58	....	3 5	
Potter's Bar	....		....	....	7 42	8 3	....	8 36	8 58	....	9 41	....	....	1034	....	....	....	1157	....	....	2 8	....	....	
Barnet ..[Hatch	....	4 55	6 16	7 16	7 50	8 10	8 27	8 44	9 7	....	....	9 52	....	1042	....	....	....	12 5	1228	1 33	2 16	....	....	3 0
Southgte & Colny	....	5 1	6 22	7 22	7 57	8 18	8 33	8 50	9 14	....	....	9 58	....	1048	....	....	....	....	1234	1 45	2 23	2 55	....	3 7
WoodGreen 1114	....	5 5	6 26	7 26	8 1	8 22	8 37	....	....	....	....	10 2	....	1052	....	....	....	....	1238	1 49	2 27	3 0	....	3 11
Hornsey	....	5 8	6 29	7 29	8 4	8 25	8 40	....	....	....	....	10 5	....	1055	....	....	....	....	1241	1 52	2 30	3 4	....	3 14
Finsbury Pk 116	....	5 12	6 33	7 33	8 8	8 30	8 44	....	....	....	....	1010	....	1059	c	....	....	....	1246	1 56	2 35	3 9	....	3 18
Holloway	3 10	5 19	6 38	7 38	8 14	8 36	8 49	9 5	9 29	9c35	10 0	1015	1037	11 4	1140	1146	1155	1220	1251	2 [illegible]	2 40	3 15	3 30	3 23
King's C. (Ter) ar	3 15	....	....	....	....	8 42	....	9 10	9 35	9 40	10 5	....	1042	11 [illegible]	1145	1151	12 0	1225	....	....	....	....	3 35	3 28
,, (York Rd)	....	....	....	7 43	8 19	8 42	8 54	9 18	9 36	9 42	10 7	1022	1111	1111	1152	1152	12 3	1228	1256	2 8	2 45	3 25	3 44	3 44
,, (Met.) dep	....	5 27	6 46	7 46	8 22	8 45	8 57	9 16	9 39	9 45	1010	1025	1114	1114	1155	1155	12 6	1231	1259	2 11	2 48	3 28	3 47	3 47
Farringdn St. arr	....	5 30	6 50	7 50	8 26	8 49	9 1	9 20	9 43	9 49	1014	1029	1118	1118	1159	1159	1210	1235	1 3	2 15	2 52	3 32	3 51	3 51
Aldersgate St. ,,	....	5 33	6 52	8 2	8 28	8 51	9 9	9 22	9 45	9 51	1016	1034	1120	1120	12 1	12 1	1212	1237	1 27	2 17	2 54	....	3 53	3 53
Moorgate St... ,,	....	5 35	6 54	8 4	8 30	8 53	9 11	9 24	9 47	9 53	1018	1036	1122	1122	12 3	12 3	1214	1239	1 29	2 19	2 56	....	3 55	3 55
Ludgate Hill.. ,,	....	....	7 19	7 53	8 43	9 0	9 4	9 30	9 54	10 1	1023	1032	1128	1128	1213	1213	....	1251	1 6	2 30	2 59	3 35	4 8	4 8
Victoria...... ,,	....	....	7 54	8 39	9 18	9 39	9 59	10 7	1028	....	11 4	1110	12 5	12 5	1248	1248	....	1 28	1 40	3 19	3 34	4 8	4 43	4 43

Hitchin .....dep		aft	aft	4 0	aft	5 15	aft	5 32	aft	aft	aft	8 7	aft	aft	9 50		2 20	8 5	8 49	aft	6 40	7 0	9 27	....
Stevenage		....	....	4 9	....	....	....	5 40	....	....	....	8 15	....	....	9 58		mrn	8 14	mrn	....	aft	7 9	aft	....
Welwyn		....	....	4 22	....	....	....	5 52	....	....	....	8 28	....	....	10 9		....	8 29	....	....	....	7 20	....	....
118 St. Albans d	Saturdays only.	....	....	4 14	....	....	....	5 25	....	....	7 54	....	....	....	9 37		....	8 10	....	5 30	....	....	....	....
Hatfield 117,118		....	....	4 35	....	....	....	6 7	....	....	8 17	8 40	....	....	1024		....	8 39	....	5 50	7 8	7 35	....	....
Potter's Bar		....	....	4 44	....	....	....	6 17	....	....	8 27	....	....	9 55	1034		....	8 50	....	....	....	7 48	....	....
Barnet ...[Hatch		4 7	....	4 53	5 32	....	....	6 25	6 50	7 28	8 35	8 55	9 31	10 2	1041	SUNDAYS.	....	9 0	....	6 4	....	7 59	....	....
Southgte & Colny		4 13	4 43	4 59	5 38	....	6 2	6 32	6 56	7 34	8 42	....	9 37	10 9	1048		....	9 8	....	6 11	....	8 10	....	....
Wood Green 1 114	3 24	4 17	4 47	....	5 42	....	6 6	6 36	7 0	7 38	8 46	....	9 41	1014	1053		....	9 13	....	6 16	....	8 17	....	....
Hornsey	3 27	4 20	4 50	....	5 45	....	6 9	6 39	7 3	7 41	8 49	....	9 44	1017	1056		....	9 17	....	6 20	....	8 21	....	....
Finsbury Pk.116	3 31	4 24	4 54	....	5 49	....	6 12	6 43	7 7	7 45	8 53	....	9 48	1021	11 1		....	9 22	....	6 25	....	8 28	....	....
Holloway	3 35	4 29	4 59	5c14	5 54	5c55	6 18	6 48	7 13	7 50	8 58	9c15	9 53	1026	11 6		3 10	9 30	9 35	6c29	7 37	8c34	10c5	....
King's C.(Ter.) ar	3 40	....	....	5 19	....	6 0	....	6 53	....	....	9 3	9 20	....	1030	....		3 15	9 35	9 40	6 34	7 45	8 39	1010	....
,, (York Rd)	....	4 34	5 5	5 30	6 0	6 6	6 23	6 57	7 18	7 55	9 3	9 31	9 58	....	1111		....	....	....	....	....	....	....	....
,, (Met.) dep	....	4 37	5 8	5 35	6 3	6 9	6 26	7 0	7 21	7 58	9 6	9 34	10 1	....	1114		....	9 38	....	6 42	....	8 45	1019	....
Farringdon St. ar	....	4 41	5 12	5 37	6 7	6 13	6 30	7 4	7 25	8 2	9 10	9 38	10 5	....	1118		....	9 42	....	6 46	....	8 49	1023	....
Aldersgate St. ,,	....	4 56	5 22	5 39	6 15	6 15	6 37	7 6	7 27	8 15	9 12	9 40	10 7	....	1120		....	9 44	....	6 48	....	8 51	1025	....
Moorgate St... ,,	....	4 58	5 24	5 41	6 17	6 17	6 39	7 8	7 29	8 17	9 14	9 42	10 9	....	1122		....	9 46	....	6 50	....	8 53	1027	....
Ludgate Hill.. ,,	....	4 44	5 15	5 57	6 10	6 26	6 33	7 18	7 35	8 5	9 28	10 8	1032	....	1143		....	10 8	....	6 58	....	9 18	1038	....
Victoria .... ,,	....	5 29	5 53	6 39	6 48	7 2	7 11	7 54	8 12	8 43	1015	1044	11 7	....	1219		....	1048	....	7 27	....	1017	1117	....

F MARCH.

, For other Trains between London and Finsbury Park, see page 116; and London and Wood Green, see page 114.

Fig. 9 Bradshaw's Railway Guide for 1873

The Luton branch was much the same as it is today (though faster in 1887) with eight trains per weekday averaging a 35 minute journey, instead of seven trains averaging 44 minutes. Also on Sundays they had two trains whereas now we have none. But on the main line there are 32 Sunday trains instead of the eight in Victorian days.

Both the St. Albans and Hertford branch lines ran shuttle services of 11 trains each way per day (and two on Sundays), and these were still running until 30th September, 1951. A new halt for Hill End Hospital was open in September, 1905, but the heyday of the St. Albans branch was during the second world war when large numbers of de Havilland workers arrived at the special platform in Lemsford Road; and—to everyone's surprise—when the new road linking the Comet roundabout to Cavendish Way was opened in 1957, a large and expensive bridge was built over the little railway line which now only has three goods trains per day, and there was even extra room left so that the railway might one day be double-tracked.

The Hertford branch, which turns off from the main line at what is now Welwyn Garden City, ran past the halt at Attimore Hall (opened May, 1905), through Cole Green and Hertingfordbury to Hertford North. In 1923 Garden Citizens complained to their newly founded local newspaper that to reach Hertford they had to travel into Hatfield in order to go back past their own wayside platform without stopping. The branch is now used for one of Hertfordshire's main industries—filling London's refuse into large holes from which gravel has been dug.

But the thing which impresses one about 1887 is that the railway station was *the one* centre of transport activity, and highly co-ordinated activity at that. At 8-05 the train arrived from Luton, at 8-06 the train from Hertford, at 8-10 the train from St. Albans, and at 8-13 the train from Hitchin which then departed at 8-15 for King's Cross. At 8-20 the train from King's Cross arrived, and departed at 8-22 for Hitchin, followed by the 8-22 train to St. Albans, the 8-23 train to Hertford, and the 8-25 train to Luton. What fun it must have been to be a signalman at the time!

The two most exciting trains of that period seem to have been the "Hertford Flyer" and the "Lord Salisbury Special" (though the names were not officially used in those days even for the 10 a.m. which later became called the "Flying Scotsman"). Until the loop-line to Hertford, via Enfield and Cuffley, was opened at long last in 1924, the fastest trains to Hertford ran via Hatfield, and the 4-30 p.m. from King's Cross, with a mere four or five coaches instead of the usual inner suburban 11 (Fig. 10) tore through Wood Green at 60 m.p.h. with the tail-end of the Stirling 0-4-4 well tank swaying wildly from side to side. Even in 1873 it reached Hatfield in 30 minutes, and Hertford in 58 minutes, times not bettered till the diesels came.

Fig. 10 Hatfield suburban train in 1900, with "somersault" signal behind

From 1870 to 1903 the most famous of all express engines were the "Stirling Eight-Foot Singles" (Fig. 11). Fortunately it is not necessary to rely on photographs or the imagination, because No. 1 is preserved in all its glory of green, gold, scarlet and black in the Railway Museum at York, well worth a visit from anyone who has (or can make) half-an-hour to spare at York in the daytime. Of course these engines were stationed only at King's Cross, Peterborough, Grantham or Doncaster, but yet here is a photograph of No. 671 (built 1882, stationed at King's Cross) in the locomotive yard at *Hatfield,* with the engine headed towards London. In those days, the third Marquis of Salisbury was Prime Minister (for the third time from 1895—1902) and nearing his 70th birthday, "and a saloon carriage was set aside for his personal use between King's Cross and Hatfield. During the Parliamentary session a top link express engine, usually an 8-footer, was kept in steam at King's Cross ready to take Lord Salisbury's saloon, and the photograph taken by Mr. Reynolds depicts No. 671 after one such trip. What days they were! One can imagine the carriage, with its immaculately groomed horses, the liveried coachman and postillion that took the Prime Minister from the station up to Hatfield House. It all seems centuries apart from our age" (from O. S. Nock, "The Great Northern Railway" Ian Allan Ltd, 1958).

[*Photo by W. J. Reynolds*

Fig. 11   The "Lord Salisbury Special" 4-2-2 at Hatfield

TRACK WIDENING AND THE LOOPLINE

The reason for the lack of progress in speeds between 1887 and 1959 was simple—nine tunnels and a big viaduct (Fig. 12) between King's Cross and Stevenage (see Fig. 5, p. 12). The six tracks north of Hatfield station look impressive (Fig. 7) but the left-hand one is the Luton branch, the right-hand one is the Hertford branch, and the remaining quadruple track was the exception rather than the rule.

From New Barnet through Hadley Wood to Potters Bar, and from Welwyn Garden City station through Welwyn to Knebworth there were only two lines of rails. Even with the chief expresses "grouped" to run together as the 9-50, 10-0, 10-5, 10-10, 10-15 and 10-20 a.m., with a gap till the 1-0 p.m. group, it was very difficult to avoid coal trains delaying passenger trains.

It was estimated in 1895 that opening out the two bottlenecks at Hadley Wood and Welwyn would cost £800,000 for a mere five route miles of railway. The alternative loop line from Wood Green through Enfield, extended by 19½ miles through Cuffley and Hertford to Stevenage (Figs. 3, 4, 7), although costing more still, was decided upon because it would tap fresh sources of business from residential traffic. It was eventually opened for passenger traffic in 1924, and Hatfield then ceased to be the important "junction for Hertford". It was also possible to by-pass Hatfield, and this was important on occasions when accidents blocked the line as at Welwyn Garden City in 1935, or during 1953—1959 when each week-end the Potters Bar tunnels and station were being widened on the direct route. There are now four tracks all the way for the 20 miles from King's Cross to Welwyn Garden City, which is the reason why the service has been improved to three comfortable trains every hour, instead of one fast one and a stopping train with engine and carriages over 40 years old.

SPEED

In the nineteenth century when there were over 12 different English and four different Scottish railway lines, each system had its own claim to fame. The L.N.W. claimed to be the most important, the G.W.R. was the longest, and the Midland the richest; the N.E.R. carried the most goods, the G.E.R. carried the most passengers; the Caledonian was famous for scenery, the S.E. & C. for the Continent, the L. & Y. for business men—but the Great Northern was the line for speed. The G.N.R. even succeeded for a while in providing the fastest service to Manchester (via Retford) and to Cambridge (via Hitchin), in spite of the routes being longer than their L.N.W. or G.E. rivals, and of course, the famous 1887 and 1895 railway races to Edinburgh and to Aberdeen depended on how fast a start the G.N. could provide.

By Hatfield an engine-driver could get his second wind after all the climbing through tunnels (Fig. 5), and on the short downhill stretch from Potters Bar to the River Lea the first high speeds would be attained before climbing again through the Welwyn tunnels to Woolmer Green summit. Train spotters have long recognized Hatfield station as a fine vantage point for watching expresses at speed, because the "up" trains are also hastening downhill and have not yet run into the tunnels or traffic troubles of the terminus. As early as 1911, Hatfield was passed at a full 80 m.p.h., but the most notable occasion must have been 27th September, 1935, when Britain's first streamlined train "The Silver Jubilee" had its trial run: Wood Green 70 m.p.h., Potters Bar 75 m.p.h., rushing through Hatfield to the valley of the Lea at 98 m.p.h. (Fig. 12), and only falling to 88 m.p.h. at Woolmer Green.

[*Daily Mirror photo*

Fig. 12   The Silver Jubilee crossing the Welwyn Viaduct

ACCIDENTS

From 1850 onwards (see p. 13) Hatfield has had its share of accidents, though they do not seem to have been caused by excessive speed. The first passenger to meet his death on the G.N.R., Mr. Francis Pym, of Biggleswade, did so at Hatfield on April 7th, 1860, when one of the Manchester "fliers" was wrecked in passing through the station. The cause was the displacement of a rail which flew up and killed a platelayer at the same time. "Unfortunately for the Company, Mr. Pym died intestate, leaving a widow and nine children and, as the property was all entailed to the eldest son, the others were legally unprovided for. Under these circumstances a jury awarded £1000 compensation to the widow, and £1500 to each child—£13,000 in all."

In 1866, on 10th June, half an hour after midnight on Sunday morning, a sensational accident occurred in the middle of Welwyn South tunnel when three goods trains came into collision. The general manager,

Mr. Seymour Clarke, was called from his bed at Hatfield and arrived at dawn to find suffocating clouds of smoke and waves of intense heat issuing from the mouth of the tunnel; there was a roar like a mighty cataract and at intervals there were explosions. One goods train going north had broken down in the tunnel; another had crashed into its rear, tossing trucks on to the "up" line (including some casks of oil), and an "up" meat train of Scotch beef had crashed into the middle of it all. A column of flame issued from the air shaft of the tunnel, eighty feet above the rails, and aroused the countryside. The only fire-engine available, a small one belonging to the Marquis of Salisbury's Hatfield estate, was despatched to the scene and by evening it was possible to enter the tunnel to bring the fire engine to the seat of the fire. Fortunately only two men lost their lives. The chief cause of the accident was inadequate signalling arrangements which were improved in consequence. (From Charles Grinley's "History of the Great Northern Railway").

In 1870, on 26th December, the breaking of a carriage tyre caused an accident at Hatfield (apparently without serious consequences), whilst the collision in January, 1878, was notable for the impetus which it gave to the introduction of continuous vacuum brakes; a goods train had broken down at Hatfield and the night "Scotsman" had run into it, but whereas a year ago at Arlesey a similar accident had caused five deaths, by now the express had been fitted with continuous brakes and its speed had been so much reduced that no passenger was seriously injured.

Accidents at Abbots Ripton and Arlesey in 1876 led to the development of the famous "somersault" signal (Fig. 10, p. 24) which snow or frost would cause to return to danger; and the insistence on a clear "sky" background for all signals needing to be sighted at high speed led to spectacularly tall signal posts, such as the one—over 50 ft. high— which carried the distant arms for the 20 mile down box N. of Hatfield.

In recent times, Welwyn Garden City has been in the news with an accident in 1935, and in 1957, on January 7th, when the overnight express from Aberdeen to King's Cross crashed into the rear of a local train, killing one person and injuring 24. But to end on a more cheerful note, let us consider the accident to that Aberdeen express mentioned on p. 4, which fortunately involved no death. At the enquiry the driver said "It rolled to the left, then to the right, and then it steadied. When she rolled, I said to the engine, 'Steady on, old girl'. She did steady but only for a moment". But the most valuable evidence came from two schoolboys who happened to be engaged at that moment in the very right and proper occupation for boys of sitting on a fence collecting engine numbers. They noticed an astonishing amount of detail (said Canon Roger Lloyd in the *Railway Magazine*) considering that the train was running past them at more than a mile a minute, so that they could have had only a few seconds for observation. "Coming round the corner the express was wobbling. The tender was going one way and the boiler another. The wobble was sideways like a snake. After the engine had passed me, the front wheels came off first, and then the two back wheels later." He saw the first carriages and the tender "going up" and leaving the lines. He looked immediately afterwards and saw that the line was no longer there. It must have been a proud moment for the two school-boys to have their pastime officially recognised as "most valuable".

ROADS IN THE TWENTIETH CENTURY

The subject of accidents (few and far between on the railway) leads naturally back to the subject of roads. In local newspapers the A.1 through Hatfield and past the Garden City is known, with reason, as the "Five Bloodstained Miles", and the number of accidents has grown steadily with the speed of the traffic. Among the many valuable lives thus cast away have been those of Michael Ventris who deciphered Linear B—the ancient Greek alphabet of Mycenae (1956), and Dennis Brain the brilliant horn-player (1957), both at the age of 36.

The roads began to resume their importance with the cycling boom from 1884 to 1900. Mr. S. C. Hankin records that one Sunday morning in 1898 a thousand cyclists (including himself) passed High Barnet Church in one hour on their way to Hatfield. From 1900 cars began to use the roads in greater numbers. From 1904 pitch from coal-tar was used to improve the road surfacing. In 1907 the very first ever A.A. Road Sign was put up at the southern end of Hatfield on the A.1000 (fig. 13). Before 1914 buses ran from Golders Green on Sunday to

[*Photo by permission of the Autocar*

Fig. 13   First A.A. Road Sign, 1907, "Doncaster 143 miles"

29

a terminus outside the One Bell. By 1922 the National Omnibus Company had established a garage in Hatfield. In 1925 a bus was running five times a day from Welwyn Garden City through Hatfield to St. Albans (Fig. 14). In 1927 the Barnet By Pass became necessary because of increased traffic, but not till 1954 was its number changed from A.555 to A.1 and a conscious effort made to divert more traffic out of Hatfield Old Town. The siting of de Havillands, together with the Green Lanes and Ellenbrook housing development on the far side of the By Pass, though probably difficult to avoid, was characteristic of the lack of planning in the "Thoughtless Thirties" for which we now have to pay the price.

For a pedestrian to cross the main stream of de Havilland-bound traffic on the A.1 at 8-45 a.m. on a weekday is a long and nerve-racking experience, though the provision of traffic islands, a roundabout at the Comet, and a 40 m.p.h. limit have helped in recent years. The obvious solution is a tunnel or bridge as proposed in the Development Corporation's Master Plan of October, 1949, instead of the present dangerous "level-crossing". What a pity that the 4th Marquis of Salisbury did not remember the obstinacy of the 2nd Marquis in 1861 and refuse to sell his land to the Development Corporation in 1948 unless a bridge or subway was built between the homes of Hatfield's people and their place of work on the opposite side of the traffic artery!

KENNETH HUTTON

POSTSCRIPT

As this book goes to press, a revolutionary road possibility is announced. On 9th November, 1960, the Minister of Transport admitted that for the past six months he had been considering a proposal from the Hertfordshire County Council to re-route 10 miles of the A.1 between the 'Clock' at Welwyn and Ridge Hill on the A.6. Presumably this new motorway would go West of both Brocket Park and the de Havilland Airfield, approximately on the extreme left-hand edge of the map on *page* 32 (Fig. 15). *If* this is ever built (and there are two alternative plans), at a cost of £5,000,000 or more and starting in 1966 or so, it would make an enormous difference to Hatfield. For the first time in 300 years, it would be off the Great North Road.

[*Photo by courtesy of the driver, Mr. Joseph Aldworth and of the "Herts Countryside"*]

Fig. 14   Welwyn Garden City—Hatfield—St. Albans Bus, 1925

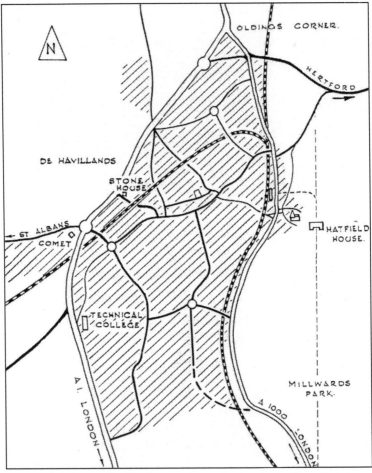

Fig. 15 Hatfield Town in 1959 between the two London Roads. (Since Book 1 was published, a new road to Hertford from the A.1000 has been made, straight across from the railway bridge, and Hatfield has obtained its first permanent traffic lights.)

Scale 1¾ inches = 1 mile.

INDEX